HOLIDAYS AND FESTIVALS

Presidents' Day

Rebecca Rissman

Heinemann Library
Chicago, Illinois

www.heinemannraintree.com

Visit our website to find out more information about Heinemann-Raintree books.

To order:

☎ Phone 888-454-2279

▣ Visit www.heinemannraintree.com to browse our catalog and order online.

Edited by Adrian Vigliano and Rebecca Rissman
Designed by Ryan Frieson
Picture research by Tracy Cummins
Leveling by Nancy E. Harris
Originated by Capstone Global Library Ltd.
Printed in China by South China Printing Company Ltd.

15 14 13 12 11 10
10 9 8 7 6 5 4 3 2 1

Library of Congress Cataloging-in-Publication Data
Rissman, Rebecca.
  Presidents Day / Rebecca Rissman.
    p. cm.—(Holidays and festivals)
  Includes bibliographical references and index.
  ISBN 978-1-4329-4056-0 (hc)—ISBN 978-1-4329-4075-1 (pb) 1.
Presidents' Day—Juvenile literature. 2. Washington, George, 1732-
1799—Juvenile literature. 3. Lincoln, Abraham, 1809-1865—Juvenile
literature. 4. Presidents—United States—History—Juvenile literature. I.
Title.
  E176.8.R57 2011
  394.261—dc22   2009052856

Acknowledgments

The author and publishers are grateful to the following for permission to reproduce copyright material: Corbis ©Bettmann **p.6**; Corbis ©Martin H. Simon **p.7**; Corbis ©Tim Pannell **p.18**; Getty Images/KarenBleier/AFP **p.5**; Getty Images **pp.15**, **23a**; istockphoto ©John Clines **p.22**; Library of Congress Prints and Photographs **pp.8**, **9**, **12**, **14**, **16**, **23b**; Shutterstock ©Morgan Lane Photography **p.4**; Shutterstock ©leigh **p.10**; Shutterstock ©Christopher Halloran **p.17**; Shutterstock ©Jaren Jai Wicklund **p.19**; Shutterstock ©Igor Karon **p.20**; Shutterstock ©Pete Hoffman **p.21**; The Bridgeman Art Library International ©Emanuel Gottlieb (1816-68)/Metropolitan Museum of Art, New York, USA **p.11**; The Granger Collection, New York **p.13**.

Cover photograph of Presidential Seal on podium in front of The White House, low angle view, USA, Washington DC, reproduced with permission of Getty Images/Joseph Sohm-Visions of America.

Back cover photograph reproduced with permission of Library of Congress Prints and Photographs.

Every effort has been made to contact copyright holders of any material reproduced in this book. Any omissions will be rectified in subsequent printings if notice is given to the publisher.

Contents

What Is a Holiday?

People celebrate holidays.
A holiday is a special day.

Presidents' Day is a holiday.
Presidents' Day is in January.

The Story of Presidents' Day

The president is the leader of the United States.

On Presidents' Day people honor all
United States presidents.

President Washington

On Presidents' Day people
remember George Washington.

George Washington was America's first president.

Before George Washington, America was ruled by the King of England.

George Washington helped America to become free.

President Lincoln

On Presidents' Day people
remember Abraham Lincoln.

Abraham Lincoln was America's
16th president.

He led America during the Civil War.
During the Civil War two parts of
14 America fought each other.

Abraham Lincoln fought to keep the country together. He fought to free slaves.

Celebrating Presidents' Day

On Presidents' Day people celebrate the presidents of the past.

And people celebrate today's president, too.

People spend time together.

People have fun outdoors.

Presidents' Day Symbols

The American flag is a symbol of Presidents' Day.

The White House is where each
new president lives. It is a symbol of
Presidents' Day.

Calendar

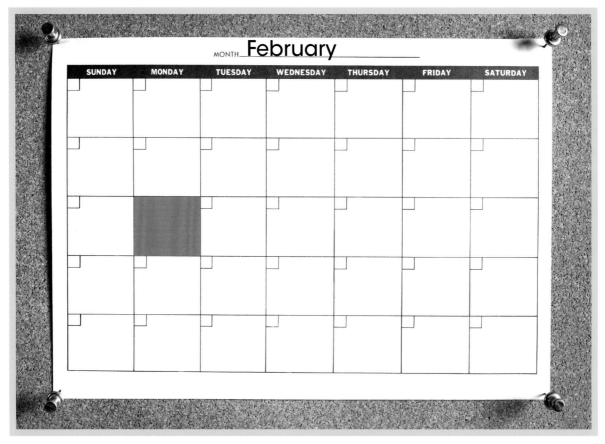

Presidents' Day is the third Monday in February.

Picture Glossary

 **slaves** people who are forced to work for no pay

 **war** a fight between two or more countries or groups

Index

Note to Parents and Teachers

Before reading

Explain that every February Americans celebrate Presidents' Day. Have a general discussion with the children around the office of president. What is the job like? What are the responsibilities? Who is the current president? Encourage the children to share all their ideas – no matter how fantastical. Briefly share some interesting facts about U.S. presidents, spanning a variety of historic periods.

After reading

Explain that Presidents' Day is also called Washington's Birthday. President George Washington was born on February 22, 1732. People use this day to remember him. Ask the children to imagine themselves as president. What would the day look like? What would they do? What laws would they like to create? There are no limits. Have them draw their impressions and share with the class.